Every Day, You Are Loved

by Michelle Schumacher

Illustrations by Maria Johnson

Copyright © 2016 Michelle Schumacher

All rights reserved.

ISBN: 0692764658

ISBN-13: 978-0692764657

For information regarding permission, please contact us at: www.michelleschumacher.com

To Chandler:
Thank you for making me the luckiest mommy in the whole world.
I love you to infinity and beyond, my dear, sweet boy.

My little one,
every day, you are loved.

You are our child,
and on our good days, our bad days,
and all our in between days,
you are loved by us,
your adoptive family.

Even if I break or lose things?

You are loved.

If I get in trouble at school for not listening to the teacher or for forgetting the rules?

You are loved.

If I play too rough and accidentally hurt someone?

You are loved.

If it's hard for me to sit still
in a restaurant or other places
where grown-ups think
I should be still?

You are loved.

If I forget that I am not supposed to tease the dog and cat?

You are loved.

If I cry and argue and fight and fuss
when I don't want to go to bed?

You are loved.

If I don't hear you when
you ask me to do something…
even if you've asked me four times?

You are loved.

If I try really hard in school
but I still don't understand?

You are loved.

If you ask me for a hug and I say no?

You are loved.

If sometimes I get really mad
and I don't even know what I'm mad
about but still I yell and struggle
when you try to hold me,
and I say mean things to you?

You are loved.

Even though I have a birth mommy
and daddy and sisters and brothers
that I still miss and sometimes
wish I was with?

You are loved by them,
and you are loved by us.

You are our child,
and on our good days,
our bad days,
and all our in between days,
you are loved by us,
your adoptive family.

Michelle Schumacher is passionate about her role as mom, foster adoption, and being the change she wishes to see in her little corner of the world in Tampa, Florida. You can learn more about her by visiting www.michelleschumacher.com.

www.ingramcontent.com/pod-product-compliance
Lightning Source LLC
Chambersburg PA
CBHW041229040426
42444CB00002B/102